The Four Winds

Small Chap Book

 # 4

Native American Poems

By

Melanie Marie Shifflett Ridner

Butterfly Woman

Contents:

Bio

Melanie Marie Shifflett Ridner

Butterfly Woman

I am a Native America Writer and Author and Poet Laureate as well as an ASCAP Songwriter .I grew up Indian and in the nineteen fifties in Dayton, Ohio, United States Of America.

I knew I was Indian and back then as children being Indian wasn't still a good thing in our history. Many health problems exist in the Indians here of today and in my Heritage.

I have several of theses medical draw backs.

But I haven't let that stop my writing or love of my people or Poetry and writing of all types. I whom cannot forsake my Heritage met a Special Bannock very educated Indian man talked with him and he became my Publisher of my first Indian Poetry Book.

My Heritage denied me by American Government was turned into a sixty page Poetry book by a man whom told me my Poetry would grace many

homes and places later on in life and that I was Indian and wise to many things is why I wrote for the Love of my people. This book is Dedicated to him who now Walks with the Spirit world as we lost Louis Hooban, a Bannock, University Professor Of Tennessee, who toured the POW WOW circles here every year till the heat killed him two summers ago. A Dear Friend and Brother whom I miss so much even more so as he knew my work would bring good medicine to our people and more.

As for me I live alone with three small dogs whom are my children. I write to keep my mind open and prey my hands stay swift to see my works travel the Continents.

I write in many different forms and work daily on this well sent gift I have been given by the old ones.

I am fifty one years old this year and love to take breaks from writing to sit and watch the butterfly's that adorn my yard for peace and rest between works.

One of our great beauty's in insect's that we have been given.

My love for the beauty and quiet fluttering and feeling the healing and peace that it gave me caused me to pick my Indian name "Butterfly Woman."

Nothing fancy for me but it could place me at such peace and calm to drift with the beautiful insect and feel such great peace and freedom to write when I needed to.

I have completed my G.E.D.education here in nineteen ninety – five and took Computer, Paralegal and Computer two year each courses by book and mind alone.

I think in the old ways I was taught by an Indian Aunt and survive well as can be expected in today's raising costs.

But Love of my Indian Heritage and many other writings have kept me writing now and for as long as the ancient ones will keep me well.

I have had sixty surgeries and one major heart attack and one heart stint inserted into the middle of my heart in March 2003, shortly after I had lost my youngest brother of the same

I whom seem to have the wise ones on my side came home to write for six more ninths when another two stints were put in side ways in my heart.

Then I sat and created this book of Love and Heritage with many other books and music for the next three years not knowing that my right side of my heart had no blood going to it. The Great Spirit showed me great kindness and strength as another four stints were put into me in an emergency heart surgery.

The Great Spirit I do believe has kept me alive for a special reason or I would not be here now.

My Indian Heritage has made me a strong woman and a survivor of many years.

My Great Grandmother lived to be one hundred and four years old and she and my Grandfather were Indians.

Our beginnings that brings me to write here today for many people here and around the world.

My goal is to have people read and enjoy and my works and Indian Heritage with me and to know always the ways of our people's and to believe we do not walk alone ever in this world ever growing and ever changing times.

I also Love to hear from many of my Brother's and Sister's and people everywhere as well.

If you have a chance to read about my works or like a special piece I do so invite people to write and also e-mail me, so I may know my works have caught your eye's mind and souls in my writings.

May the Great Spirit Guide All Everywhere

Melanie Marie Shifflett Ridner

2318 Hamilton Eaton Road

Lot # 71

Hamilton, Ohio

45011-9056

United States

melanieridner@cinci.rr.com

Many Thanks to Gordon Dellar BlackFeather, and his wife , Walks Softly whom believed in my works and whom help them to travel the world.

Please visit www.blackfeathertradingpost .com for all your

Indian needs and

many other fine works.

Melanie Marie Shifflett Ridner

Butterfly

Turquoise Faith

Turquoise, blue beauty dropped from the sky,

as a keepsake stone,

for all our tribes to have a piece of.

Beauty, to shape and treasure, in our hearts.

A gift to us to always remember our skies.

Indian Lore

I sit tonight, in the council of fire, listening to our tribal lore.

I, as little Butterfly sit to gather thoughts on what each brave brings to council..

This discussion sees us many moons ahead.

Our braves, always smart and strong.

They strong know better how to make our tribes stronger.

Every word taken into account, and every motion recorder for future generations to come, in our Indian Lore.

Falling Star

My Cherokee love is Falling Star.

So named at his birth.

Because the stars fell many that moon.

That smile, so beautiful, in that proud dark face .His heart, so kind and open.

So tall, so magnificent.

I watch him from under lashes of deep love, eyes only for my love, Falling Star.

Cherokee Child

Patience, my Cherokee Child

Round face, so full of laughter.

Enjoy your young life, because soon you'll be grown.

Listen well, to all that is taught.

Grow strong, brave and true.

With our culture we teach you.

So, for now, run and be at peace.

Our Braves

Look, women of the village!

Our braves prepare for the hunt.

How magnificent they are for the hunt.

How magnificent they are!

Spirit they have!

The buffalo run many, and we must keep up with our braves.

As they bring the giant beast down, we must be quick at our work.

As each falls from the arrows straight, we must drop to our knees quickly,

and skin in groups.

Blankets for our wigwams.

Meat for the tribe.

Our Braves will tell of this hunt for many moons to come!

Culture of the Tribe

Our culture is our way.

The Indian way of life.

The forests, our front rooms.

The valley's our kitchens.

The rivers, our nectar.

The buffalo, our food.

Our way of life is simple.

A way the white – eyes don't understand.

Valley of Pain

We are on a lonely journey, men, women, children and old ones.

Our braves have lost their pride for the moment.

Our women weep; children quiet; old ones searching for wisdom.

We are traveling the Valley of Pain.

Our hearts break on this journey.

For we are never to return to our beautiful valley.

We, the people who are so lost.

We have to move because we are being pushed out of our lands, like cattle.

We travel on, knowing what's ahead.

All praying for peace, as is our way of life.

But, our prayers are all we have on this journey.

Passing Heart

As I sit in my wigwam, on my knees, doing these blankets,

I sit and with bowed head, think of Piercing Heart.

My child of my heart.

He has left for his dream quest.

To return a man.

On his dream quest, he will take many journeys', only to return a new brave in name.

If he survives his quest, tell you he will, in the circle of fires.

I, as many women, wait in patience for his return.

No matter what, this child – man will always be my heartstrings.

Little Dove Wings

(An Indian Prayer)

Great Sachem:

I pray for Little Dove Wings.

Guide her in the many moons to come.

Keep her strong.

Breathe life into her peaceful soul.

Help her to survive our way of life.

Help her to preserve all customs, and pass them on to her children to come.

And Great Sachem,

Help her in keeping honor to our tribes....

Forever.

Shaman

Great Indian Shaman, hear my prayers:

You who watch over this tribe.

Peace and strength I ask, for my brothers and sisters.

Keep our paths safe in all journeys.

Keep our rivers and valleys to fruitfulness.

Let our children grow and multiply for our nation.

We honor your words and wisdom,

Great Shaman.

We Are Indian

We are Indian.

A long standing nation.

A brave people.

Our skins dark.

Our eyes black onyx.

Our hair thick and long.

Our bodies thin. with ways we've grown accustomed to.

The land ours.

Strong, proud, peaceful.

We've been here many suns.

We've grown a lot.

But our ways are the same.

We are Indian.

Sacred Ground

No little one, we may not cross.

This is Sacred Ground.

Only our wise ones may come and go.

For spirits guard our dead.

We must pass by with peace in our hearts.

For this is Sacred Ground.

Land Of Shawnee

Mountains high above lush forests.

Fields Of corn grown sacredly.

Running waters full of fish.

Mountains full of hunting.

Swift doe and buck.

Eagles on the sky.

Mists that meet the sun.

Howls that greet the moon.

Our land so vast that none can follow all.

Many are the Shawnee.

Our lands stretch far.

Our people live on.

Shawnee

Little Bird

Today is a day to rejoice in the tribe.

“Little Bird “has come into the world.

She is so tiny.

My hand huge against her skin.

So tiny and yet all Indian.

My “Little Bird” fluttered so inside me.

Never kicking as one would.

Just gentle flutters till born.

Sing to her I did all the time.

Now here she is, small but beautiful.

What more could an Indian Mother wish for?

I welcome my daughter.

“Little Bird”.

Days Gone By

Visions past.

Future's told.

The Indian lives on.

Survived they have.

Hardships many.

The time is now.

Recognized we will be.

Future told.

Visions now.

All come forth.

This is the Indians Day.

Mountain Journey

The mountain range is before us.

Our journey long.

We travel from the Carolinas.

Venturing across the continent.

Our beginnings in Virginia.

Our tribes extended now everywhere.

Ohio, Tennessee, Kentucky and even West were many walked "The Trail Of Tears".

Cherokee alone it was not.

Many mixed Indian Blood went.

The Indian Nations stripped and separated.

Never defeated.

Here we stand on our lands once more.

Our mountain journey begins again.

Fore Father's

Told centuries before.

Our fore father's told of all to come.

The white man came.

Our way of life destroyed.

Tree's cut and destroyed.

The buffalo almost extinct.

Our lands took.

Whiskey given to destroy our young warriors.

Our tribes abused.

Our fore father's saw all.

All was told and more.

Yes we were weak, but now the blood of thousands runs alive once more.

Yes, the fore father's saw.

They saw centuries a head as well.

The Fore Father's and prayer's of millions live on strong today.

Carolina‘s Beauty

Years ago a trip I took.

Deep into Cherokee , North Caroline.

My Indian roots screaming at such beauty as we crossed the mountains

into the Valley.

Intoxicating were my ancestors.

The Indian people so kind and open.

As I turned all four corners I saw as much as I could .

I for one would have fought for such lands as my ancestors did.

Beauty and lush green.

The land beckoned me.

Voices from long ago spoke to my soul.

In leaving , tears came to my eyes .

This was my first and no doubt last journey to my Indian Roots.

It captured my soul for eternity .

Carolina’s , Indian Beauty.

Strong Bow

Tall my Indian brave stands.

Wide his shoulders are.

His hair parted and black as the crow that flies high on the winds.

Swift he can move.

Kindness , yet strength rises from his body.

A warrior indeed.

His coups many.

The wise one's taught him well.

Strong Bow an Indian of means.

Many a maiden looks upon him.

I know I am the one he seeks.

I , "Little Otter" will make robes.

He will come for me soon.

We will be one on our journey of life.

Soon…

My brave , soon , Strong Bow.

Medicine Woman

Healer of the people .

Strong medicines I am taught.

Favored by the wise ones.

Blessed by the Spirit World.

Many I have healed.

My inner spirit guides me in all .

Heal all I do.

Roots, berries, and herbs I hunt daily for my tribe.

My work well known and never done.

Healing many of my peoples.

I am Medicine Woman .

The Four Winds

7

Multiple Mini-Series

Chap Books

By

Melanie Marie Shifflett Ridner

Native American Author

Published by :

Indian Heritage Council

Morristown , TN 37816

ISBN Number : 1-884710-42-5

New Mini-Versions

7 Book Mini- Series

"Dedicated"

To him in his memory.

A Bannock Indian Brother whom is dearly missed.

Published By :

Melanie Marie Shifflett Ridner

Native American Poet and ASCAP Songwriter

Author / Novelists

Story Teller / Chap Book Author

7 X's ASCAPlus Award Winner

www.ingramcontent.com/pod-product-compliance
Ingram Content Group UK Ltd.
Pitfield, Milton Keynes, MK11 3LW, UK
UKHW051135260726
13967UKWH00010B/3068